More of the Same

More of the Same

*Further poems and thoughts on the
Christian faith & life in general*

Stewart French

authorHOUSE®

AuthorHouse™
1663 Liberty Drive
Bloomington, IN 47403
www.authorhouse.com
Phone: 1-800-839-8640

First published by AuthorHouse   10/21/2011

ISBN: 978-1-4567-8376-1 (sc)
ISBN: 978-1-4567-8377-8 (ebk)

Printed in the United States of America

This is my second book, much along the lines of the first one: "From Heaven and Back Again". Once again I must thank all those, human and divine, Christian and non-Christian, who have guided, led, listened to, and encouraged me over the years, and who have been there in good times and the hard times. Special thanks must go to my late parents, and to my children, but most of all to my wife, Gwen, who has always been a tower of strength, and is constant in all ways. Some years ago I saw a book dedication by Dr. W.E. Sangster: "To my wife, with whom it is as easy to stay in love as it was to fall in love" - and I couldn't put it better.

Sometimes I can work through my feelings, my theology, and my problems (both domestic and work related) whilst sitting with a blank piece of paper. On other occasions a flash of inspration can sit on my computer for over a year before I move beyond the first line. I simply ask that, if anything here helps you (in any small way) to answer any of your questions, or to solve any of your problems, you thank God for it because I believe that He is the one who provided these words, not me.

Should you wish to contact the author please email to Stewartfrench-poetry@hotmail.co.uk.

FOREWORD BY LT. COL. TIM COURTENAY OBE

"ANOTHER MAN'S FLOWERS"

I left Carmarthen railway station on my first posting to 42 Commando,Royal Marines in Singapore in 1961, and my parents gave me a small paperback book of poems entitled "Other Men's Flowers". This is a compilation of poems assembled, and we are told, remembered by heart by Field Marshal Lord Wavell. This book stayed with me through the little known campaigns in the jungles of The Far East. Sadly my small book became the victim of the damp and humid climate and was last seen floating away, page by page down some swollen Borneo river in 1964.

I never replaced it until I found a copy in a second hand bookshop in the 1990s, this I treasure and read and reread whenever the spirit takes me.

I first met Stewart and Gwen when they came on a battlefield tour which I led for Bath University Staff in 2009. I took them to the Ypres Salient and the Somme. Of the many fields of battle, Passchendaele is one of the most evocative and to visit the last resting place of over 11,000 men at Tyne Cot has to be the most poignant reminder of man's inhumanity to man. Here over 60% of the bodies are unidentified and their headstone inscriptions read "A Soldier of the Great War" and beneath, the words "Known unto God".

Clearly this affected Stewart in such a way that he was moved to write his poem "Some Mother's Son". Fittingly, he first read this standing by the headstone of Lieutenant Noel Hodgson MC one of the Great War poets who lost his life in this "The war to end all wars", he lies buried in The Devonshire Trench on the Somme.

Stewart's ability to sum up his feelings and those around him is a unique gift and to have met him and discovered his talent as a poet, has for me been both uplifting and invigorating. That I have been able to give him inspiration to write further is most humbling.

I found my niche late in life, taking people to the battlefields and cemeteries of the two world wars, reminding them of the ultimate sacrifice paid by so many thousands of young people and to ensure that we never forget the words in John McCrae's poem "In Flanders Fields," that "If ye break faith in us who died we shall not sleep", and Stewart's lines are reinforcing and reminding us of our responsibilities with this great gathering of poems, truly written from the heart.

I commend this his second book of poems, but do please find a quiet corner, "Make Time" and absorb and ponder his evocative and gentle turns of phrase and the power of prayer through the lines of his poetry.

Lieutenant Colonel Tim Courtenay,
Hemyock, Devon. Easter Day 2011

Index

HOW GREAT THOU ART, HOW GREAT THOU ART

COME, NOW IS THE TIME TO WORSHIP

PRECIOUS MEMORIES

"He's got the whole world in His hands
He's got the whole wide world in His hands
He's got the whole world in His hands
He's got the whole world in His hands"

Traditional

CREATION: FROM GOD'S POINT OF VIEW

Very early one morning in 2004, when sleep just would not come, I was thinking about the Creation, and I wondered how God might tell the story . . . I realise that this is not 100% the order as described in Genesis, but it is how it came to me . . .

In the beginning there was only me. I AM from eternity past, and I AM to eternity ahead.

I looked. Nothing. Only emptiness.

So I created the heavens and the earth - shapeless and without any living thing, in perpetual darkness until I provided light. You do not need to know how I provided it, that is my secret, but believe me, it was no accident. As the unformed world turned, even as it does now, there was light, and there was darkness, there was day and there was night.

There was a lot of water - this was essential as you are 90% water, and the surface of your world is 70% water. I made the dry land to appear in the midst of the sea, in order that you would have somewhere to live.

I knew that you would need food so I provided plants of incredible complexity and variation, plants of beauty. Plants with seeds and plants bearing fruit, and I established them long before I lovingly made you.

I love beauty, and because I knew you would as well I wanted you to be aware of the bigness of my creation, so I gave you the sun, and the moon, and the stars to gaze on, and wonder. But you mean more to me than any star or any sun.

As I wanted my world to have variety - so you would have pleasure in what you see - I next created, for you, the birds and the fish: to see, to eat, and to enjoy. Likewise I made animals - the wild animals and those you would come to domesticate and use for food, and whose skins you would use for clothing. My world was now ready for you.

I knew what I wanted when I made you. Someone to care for their world. Someone who would love others I made, and who would be in fellowship with me. Someone with my characteristics of goodness, honesty and truth. I took all the love I had to spare, and I made you, my cherished one. I brought you into this universe, onto this world I had made especially for you to enjoy, and to protect. I even made allowance for the fact that you would lose your innocence and so I became one like you. I felt your fears, I understood your temptations, and I showed you how to live.

My child: all that I have ever done, I have done especially for you - won't you come home?

Yours, with love

God

*

CHOCOLATE CROISSANTS ETC

In June 2003 I was sitting in a service station, on my way to a meeting: surrounded by food, drink and discarded newspapers I started to think of the disparity between the aspirations of those of us who live in the rich West, and those in the poorer parts of the world.

"Chocolate croissants, coffee, tea. Things I want to `pleasure` me."
"Growing rice, picking tea. Things I do to sustain me."

"A bigger house, a better car, will show I have arrived."
"A scrap of bread, a cup of rice, with these I might survive."

"A second bath, or Jacuzzi, please, to make my life complete."
"All I want is a place to sleep, and something I can eat."

"Running water - hot and cold. A shower, bath and sink."
"Water that's clean is just a dream: pollution's what I drink."

"A new TV and video; a DVD's a must!"
"My home is on a rubbish tip - and I choke on clouds of dust."

"Give me more or I'll go on strike, for that's my legal right."
"Please let me have a living wage. I'll work all through the night."

"My clothes are old - they're last year's style. I'm getting out of date."
"I'm naked, and I'm hungry: does this have to be my fate?"

"All my money is tied up - there's nothing I can spare."
"Look after others, help them live, and show them that I care.

The blood I shed is not reserved for the rich and well - to - do;
I love the poor and starving ones, and you must love them too.
I gave you life, and gave you wealth, so listen when I call.
Can you see my bloodstained cross and say that "I surrender all?
All to Thee, my precious Saviour, I surrender all"?"

*

I'M SITTING IN MY RUBBISH DUMP

This sat on my PC, unfinished, for several months until I came across it again in the aftermath of the Tsunami in 2005. The last verse came to me as a response to the terrible loss suffered by so many living in a poverty I cannot imagine.

I'm sitting in my rubbish dump, my clothes are filthy rags;
I have no food today to help me live.
And Jesus sits beside me as He did whilst on this earth
When He gave all He had that He could give.

He understands my problems, caring for my awful plight.
He feels my pangs of hunger every day.
He knows my needs for clothes and food are well within my reach -
Or would be if you didn't turn away.

With Jesus in the mire with me, sharing my pain and thirst
How can you turn and look the other way?
Ignoring me is cowardice, but you cannot face the facts
For there's a serious price you'd have to pay.

You'd have to face reality, and open up your eyes;
You'd have to take the risk of finding out
Just what it means to live like this, existing without hope,
Forever one condemned to go without.

We survive by scavenging, on what the rich discard.
Surviving, but not living. Life is Hell.
Each sunrise means another day: will we see it to its end?
Do we want to? Have you thought of that as well?

A meaningless existence, we're discarded and ignored
Abandoned and forgotten so it seems.
Our lives are mere statistics and our deaths are seldom mourned:
And all we ever had were hopes and dreams.

*

CONSTANT CHANGE IS HERE TO STAY

I sometimes get angry at the way of the world. The way we are pressurised to `advance`, whilst leaving behind those unable to keep up with the latest technological changes is simply one issue that annoys me. The memories stirred by November 11th, and by the coming of Christmas surely give us reasons to reflect that some things which are eternal and precious should not be forgotten, or rushed.

I was stuck for a conclusion until, on September 10th 2004 Gwen read out from her Bible study notes a bit about the arrogance of man in the face of scientific advances, and it fell into place.

Constant change is here to stay.
"It's evolution" people say.
Old traditions, things we know -
Everything has got to go!
"The past is dead. Forget. Advance.
The future's yours, so take a chance.
Develop skills. Discover things.
See what prosperity that brings"

    "Did I hear right? I'm not sure;
    Don't people matter any more?
    The old, the folk who gave so much
    Don't matter now they're out of touch?"

"But can't you see? We must evolve.
So many issues we must solve.
Like hunger, hatred, famine too
There always seems so much to do.
Time is pressing, deadlines loom.
There is no time left. There's no room
For those who lag, who can't maintain
Our faster pace. Move on, again."

"Did I hear right? I'm not sure;
Don't people matter any more?
The old, the folk who gave so much
Don't matter now they're out of touch?"

"They're history now, the future's ours
For science gives us many powers
To change the world, to put things right -
It could almost happen overnight
If we leave behind those we don't need,
Who cannot cope with greater speed.
Forget the weak, ignore the old.
Advance. Go forward. Strong and bold."

"Did I hear right? I'm not sure;
Don't people matter any more?
The old, the folk who gave so much
Don't matter now they're out of touch?"

"They don't matter, never mind,
We have to leave the past behind.
Discard the things that hold us back
Everybody: get on track.
We are advancing, that's the key
To find our final destiny -
Which we will reach with our own hand.
Utopia: the Promised Land."

  "Did I hear right? I'm not sure;
  Don't people matter any more?
  The old, the folk who gave so much
  Don't matter now they're out of touch?"

"Forget the old, I'm telling you,
For we have got so much to do.
They've had their time. They're useless now,
And everyone must die somehow.
We must take hold and boldly clasp
The future lying in our grasp.
And boldly tread where none has trod
Then we will take the place of God."

  "Did I hear right?"

*

GOD IS CALLING YOU

In April 2003 Gwen and I went to Kosova for just under a week with SMILE International, to whom this is dedicated. Permission is also given to Jan and Steve Worthy to use these lyrics at any time.

What we saw had a great impact on me. Nothing could have prepared me for what I heard from those who survived the suffering. The answer to the world's needs lies with those who are prepared to get out of the boat, and leave their comfort zone.

God is calling you to serve Him, He is calling you by name,
And once you leave your comfort zone, you will never be the same.
Once you put Him to the test, and let Him have His way with you
Stand back and watch the Father work. Look and see what God can do.

You cannot work in your own strength, nor succeed in your own way;
But step aside and trust in Him, let Him lead you day by day.
Let His Spirit flow within you, let Him show you what is planned.
Let Him open doors before you, then just obey the Lord's command.

You may be called to serve your Lord by opening your door
To house the lonely and the sad, the widow and the poor.
To show the love of Christ to those who need to share their fears:
To let them open up their hearts, so God can heal them through their tears.

You may be called to intercede, to call on the Lord for those
In situations you can't see, but are which the Father knows.
A prayer of faith from faithful folk can change things far away.
The Father listens to His own, so make the time to pray.

You may be called to foreign lands, to places laid to waste:
With menfolk killed, and women raped, and whole villages displaced.
The hatred sown by years of war, for religion or for land,
Cannot be healed by man alone, but by God's almighty hand.

If you are called to war-torn lands, are you emotionally prepared
To sit beside the orphan, and the angry, and the scared?
Despite the reconstruction there is nothing can disguise
The widows' haunted faces, or the children's pleading eyes.

So let the Saviour lead you by the Spirit birthed within.
Each journey starts with just one step - let your journey now begin.
Step out in faith and hold God's hand, the Father's calling you:
So follow in His footsteps, and be amazed at what He'll do.

*

AN ODE TO CLIVE DOUBLEDAY

This also is the result of our trip to Kosova - albeit a bit more light-hearted. It was performed at the "end of week concert" before we left to come home.

To put things in context:-

Gjakove (pronounce Gjakova) is the town where we stayed for the week.
Clive Doubleday is (along with his wife, Ruth) the founder of SMILE International, with whom we went.
"Mir Deeta" is Albanian for "Good Morning".
Shaun Pilling is an Australian evangelist, whom God called to work in Kosova.
Jan and Steve (Worthy) are musical missionaries, playing a mixture of gospel and rock and roll to the children in Kosova and elsewhere.
And finally "Fleah" is the local dish of honour, equivalent to rolling out the red carpet: we were most honoured to be given Fleah by the locals on more than one occasion during our time in Kosova - a week I'll not forget in a hurry.

We've walked around Gjakove with our Bibles in our hands.
We've walked around Gjakove doing what dear Clive commands.
At the end of our first day each one felt we could greet a Native Kosovorian with a passable "Mir Deeta".

We left from Gatwick Airport in that land so far away.
Leaving friends and churches who had promised they would pray.
There were mixed emotions ranging from excitement through to fear -
But mainly, though the feeling was "God! What am I doing here?"

We were billeted in several homes, most sleeping on the flooring,
And somehow most of us slept through the deafening sound of snoring.
My only gripe - you may concur - I never could get used `ter
Being wakened before dawn by that noisy, crowing rooster.

We have visited the lonely and gone in to several schools.
To those who don't know Jesus we're a bunch of holy fools.
But by sitting with the widow, and giving that home a coat of paint
In the eyes of Him who counts, each person here's a saint.

Some of us are still quite deaf from those noisy sing-alongs.
With Jan and Steve, all full of life, belting out those songs
The core of which is Jesus Christ - with the banner of truth unfurled -
The only song I'm waiting for is "Rocking All Over The World".

Each one has been affected, and we have all shed many tears -
Both those of us who have grey hairs, and those of tender years.
We teamed up here with Shaun and friends, who bring hope amidst the bombs.
Who'd have thought an Aussie'd work with a load of wingeing Poms?

So now it's back to England, to our churches and our friends.
But we've been on a journey, and it's one that never ends.
So when we get to Heaven - when it's our turn to arrive
We'll save a plate of Fleah for you - **for you deserve it Reverend Clive!**

*

In loving memory of the April 2003 trip to Kosova.

THE LAND OF ISRAEL TODAY

This was written sometime in 2002 whilst I was trying to get my head around why the Middle East always seems to be in turmoil.

There's the sound of gunfire raging in the land of Jesu's birth:
There's the sound of mothers weeping for their dead.
There's a ghastly "déjà vu" about the scenes we see each day:
Not Herod's troops, but tanks and guns instead.

There's the sound of battle raging in the land that Jesus loves,
Where Jew and Arab will not coexist.
Where suicidal bombers cause such carnage in the streets
And the innocent are powerless to resist.

Yet both sides claim descent from a common Patriarch;
Both claiming Abrahamic ancestry.
So why the bloody battles, and why not the way of peace?
To us it seems a total mystery.

Could it be their understanding of the line of their descent?
Could it also be what's written in their law?
The Torah tells of Isaac as the child his father loved,
Whilst Ishmael was the child the slave girl bore.

The Koran tells another story of the fate of these two babes,
Affirming Ishmael as his father's one true son.
All Arab races, they believe, descend from Ishmael
And the Jewish race from the rejected one.

But there are many common teachings in their different Holy Books,
With the Koran teaching tolerance and love.
Whilst still affirming Islam as the perfect way of life
It respects the Jewish view of God above.

But these words have now been twisted and they are taken to extremes:
Each text is now a pretext without debate.
Which is why the land of Israel is once more awash with blood:-
For the Devil has filled either side with hate.

*

SOME MOTHER'S SON

In 2009 Gwen and I joined with members of the University of Bath Staff Association in visiting the battlefields of the Somme and Passchendaele from World War 1, under the inspired, and inspiring, leadership of Colonel Tim Courtenay.
Like so many before me, I was struck by the futility of it all, and by the loss of so many men who were each "Some Mother's Son"

White tombstones by the thousand from every race on earth,
And every one is for a son some Mother brought to birth.
Beneath the Cross of Sacrifice and the Great Crusader's Sword
Some stones have names engraved thereon, their memory secured.

But other graves hold unknown bones, "A Soldier known to God";
You lie in serried ranks in death as you rest beneath the sod.
You did not start this dreadful war, but you chose to face the gun.
We may not know your name, my friend, but you were some Mother's son.

*

The rights for this poem are given to the Royal British Legion in perpetuity.

ONLY GOD WOULD KNOW

This also was written during a battlefield tour, this time in 2010, when we went to visit the scenes of the D day landings, again under the leadership of Colonel Tim Courtenay who has the gift of conveying the reality and the horror of war without ever making it sound glamorous.

They came from many nations to fight the common foe,
But who would live, and who would die, only God would know.
The many gravestones, line on line, show the scale of those who died,
But cannot show the ones that lived, with all their scars inside.

They did not flinch from danger, though they all knew real fear:
They came to do their duty, for they held their country dear.
The carnage all around them, from mine, and bomb and shell
Transformed the peaceful landscape into a scene from Hell.

We stand among the fallen, for this is hallowed ground:
But what about the missing, those whose bones were never found?
We honour all the fallen, from air, and sea, and land
And what they saw before they died, we will never understand.

These men from many nations who were united in one cause
Had come to fight for freedom`s sake in just one of many wars.
But there are dead from other nations, now our friends but then the foe:
And who would live? And who would die? Only God could know.

*

Recited in Ranville Cemetery March 2010

The rights for this poem are given to the Royal British Legion in perpetuity.

A MILLION IS A STATISTIC

Gwen and I did not go on the battlefield tour in 2011, but this came to me whilst I was thinking about the previous 2 tours we had been privileged to join. The title comes from a line in the poem, which was a quote by Joseph Stalin.

The battlefield lays silent, where bullets no longer fly:
And all that's left are rows of graves of those who came to die.
All seems so very tranquil in this cemetery of rest
As we give thanks for those who died, whose memory is blessed.
We can stand and gaze in reverence at each and every grave
Which marks the final resting place of one who came, and gave.

Across the world, in other lands, the same does not apply.
Bombs are dropped, and rockets land, and deadly bullets fly.
Mines are laid, and mines explode, the noise of battle rages,
Lives are lost, and people maimed, not named on history's pages.
"A single death is tragedy" - but Stalin was realistic -
He also said "A million deaths is purely a statistic".

Why do nations go to war, why must people die in battle?
Why must we try to overcome, and hear those sabres rattle?
In many cases young men fight to right a perceived wrong:
To stand up for their father's faith, or for the land where they belong.
The country calls them to the flag, to hold truth's banner high:-
The call is made, and men respond, and many people die.

The bullet holes in many homes, and the craters in the road;
The shell-shocked faces of the folk who'd seen the bombs explode.
Afraid of waking up at dawn, and afraid at close of day,
Afraid this the war will never end, afraid this Hell won't go away.
Praying often, praying hard, that one day the bombs will cease,
And let their children play again, when their land has peace.

*

2010

**"One day at a time, sweet Jesus
That's all I`m asking from you.
Lord, give me the strength to do every day
What I have to do."**

Words by Marijohn Wilkins

TAKE THE PAIN

A group of us had been praying for several months for a friend to be healed. We finally got the news that she had died on Tuesday 22 Feb 2001. During the sharing of memories and a prayer time that evening there was a period of quiet, during which I could almost feel the pain her widower was going through, and the words he may need to offer to God. I hope that it may help someone who needs to express pain at such a time.

Take the pain that I am feeling,
Take the hurts within my soul.
Through the fog of my confusion
Jesus - will You make me whole?

Take the loneliness that beckons,
Take the years that lie ahead.
Give me strength to face the future.
Jesus - do what You have said.

Stay beside me as I'm grieving,
Stay beside me and be still.
You have promised not to leave me:
Jesus - I embrace Your will.

*

ALONE - IN A CROWD

Despite being a Christian for many years, there are times when feelings from my past come back and affect the way I react. I wrote this during a training course when I could see all the other managers laughing and joking - and I could not bring myself to join in.

There's a crowd of people around me;
Happy faces, happy voices, all talking.
I'm alone, I'm unknown, and I'm lonely -
I want to walk, and just keep on walking.
Away from this sea of faces, away from the babble of noise,
Away, where I feel accepted, with my collection of toys.
Toys that remind me of safety, that transport me back to the past -
When I was safe in the bosom of family.
Why couldn't that feeling still last?

In this place I feel I don't matter
When I'm alone in the crowd.
I want to break into their circle
But I know that I won't be allowed.
I'm an insignificant person, with nothing of value to share.
So why would anyone bother? Why would anyone care?
If I walked out the door from this gathering
I know I would never be missed.
I'm just an invisible person
On nobody's "favourites" list.

*

SPIRIT TOUCH ME

I often find in times of difficulty or stress that I can work out my feelings, and give them over to God by putting them down in poetry. The opening lines of this had sat on our computer for months, but at around two o'clock one morning, when sleep was just a forlorn hope, the rest took shape, and I went back to bed in a far better frame of mind.

Spirit touch me, Spirit lead me; Spirit do your work within.
Spirit reach me, Spirit free me; Spirit cleanse me from all sin.
Make me free to serve the Father: make me whole and make me pure:
Open up my mind, I beg you, so I know His plans for sure.

Spirit guide me, Spirit show me; show the Father's perfect will.
Spirit calm me, Spirit help me; let my mind rest and be still.
Help me sit in contemplation listening to the Father's word:-
Ears attuned to what He's saying, then obeying what I've heard.

Spirit feed me, Spirit teach me all I need to understand.
Spirit help me, Spirit touch me; I need to feel your gentle hand
Giving constant reassurance of the Father's love and care.
For sometimes in the midst of trouble - I simply need to know you're there.

*

November 2003

ARE YOU LISTENING?

We know we are encouraged to "Praise God in all circumstances", and often we can do so, although just as the Psalmist sometimes found the situations he encountered overpowering and overwhelming, so can we today. Family, friends, work, money (or lack of it) and many other circumstances can all bring us to a point of desperation. God encourages us to pour out our feelings to Him, as it is only when we are honest that He can deal with us. This was written in September 2001.

Are You listening whilst I'm speaking? Do You hear a word I say?
Are You looking at me, Father, or have You turned Your face away?
How can You be indifferent when You've told us we must pray?
How can You? God?

Don't You know my needs are pressing? Don't You know my fears are great?
My concerns are overwhelming. Time is pressing - I can't wait.
I can't maintain perspective, I'm in a very screwed-up state.
Please help me! God!

The pressures are all crowding me, coming in from every side.
And nothing seems to settle me; no matter what I've tried.
It's getting worse. I just can't sleep. I'm really petrified!
Please help me! God!

Why is my life so difficult, and why is life so hard?
Why can't I be like all the rest, and be `dealt a decent card`?
If this is now, what lies ahead? Will I be forever scarred?
Please help me! God!

Is there any way out of this Hell? Any further I can fall?
Is life really worth the living now? Why don't I simply end it all?
If I decide to end it now, would You hear me if I call?
Well? Would You? God?

Would You really care about me then? Or would You turn Your back again?
Just like it seems You're doing now, when I'm feeling so much pain.
Do You really have a clue about the turmoil in my brain?
Well? Do You? God?

*

GIVE IT ALL TO GOD

Why is it that the theory is often so much easier than the practice? In October 2002 I had deadlines looming at work, major customers crying out for information, and not enough time (so I thought) to obtain it all. Between the hours of 1.30 and 5.30 in the morning I couldn't rest, and between reading the Bible, and pacing up and down whilst trying to pray, I wrote this.

My mind is spinning endlessly, it will not let me rest:
With thoughts of work, and worries that I can't get off my chest.
The things that I should leave behind, as I close the office door
Are coming home with me again, and disturb my sleep once more.

Why don't I trust my God enough to give Him all my fear?
Why won't I give these thoughts to Him, then let my God draw near?
Why do I put my darling wife through these nights of broken sleep
When God is waiting patiently? It's enough to make me weep.

"Cast your burdens on to me" is what our Saviour said.
"Don't fear about tomorrow, just ask for your daily bread.
Your Father knows your every need, and He knows each anxious thought.
He has your future in His hands" is what our Saviour taught.

So when I'm tossing sleeplessly, with deadlines looming large
I should remember what He said: "The Father is in charge."
It's easy when I think like that to tell Jesus "Take it all"
It's easy then - in theory. But I am human after all.

*

And yes, I did manage to get it all done.

LIVING IN THE FAST LANE

Another poem that came early one morning when I was feeling the pressure at work: "Thank You, Lord, that I can express my worries and fears on paper, and You consider them prayers! - and thank You Lord for my wife and for friends who listen non-judgementally"

I am living my life in the fast lane!
I cannot relax or unwind!
Adrenaline flowing, rough edges are showing
And ever unsettling my mind.

My life is so full of deadlines
With myriads of targets to meet,
That I make no time now for Jesus:
To pray, or to sit at His feet.

I must meet each new set of targets,
I must reach those standards now set.
I can't get off from this treadmill
With so many targets not met.

And when I have met my objectives
There's another appraisal that's due.
A new set of targets, and figures
"To develop and motivate you".

Is this all there is in the future?
High pressure. "We're raising the bar
To seek out those highest achievers
And those who we think will go far".

We each have our gifts and our talents
With which we have all been endowed;
To be used to their best in the workplace
So we can stand out from the crowd.

But not at the cost of our family.
But not if Christ is ignored.
In all that we do, at home or at work
Remember, that Jesus is Lord.

He is Lord of the workplace and family;
He's involved in all that we do.
So I must give Him the chance to refresh me
And allow for His peace to break though

*

March 2004

IS THERE ANY PURPOSE?

In early 2004 I was feeling the pressure at work: a new regime, constant deadlines, and - I felt - unrealistic expectations. Around the time I was writing this I had a long talk one day with Suzanne, a lady at work, and just talking helped put things into perspective - which has survived for the last 7 years, so "Thank you" Suzanne.

I have tried, repeatedly, to add something more at the end, to `round it off`, but I cannot find the words - so I just leave it that my wife, Gwen, has always been an absolute tower of strength. With her by my side, and with God in the picture as well, there is always hope.

Is there any real purpose in my slaving all day long?
To never getting credit, only blame if things go wrong?
To feel the constant pressure to succeed what `ere the cost?
When all that seems to matter is "profits won and profits lost"?

Is there really any purpose to having constant targets set?
To know that they'll be raised again the minute that they're met?
To know that past achievements count for nothing now they're gone?
Each day, afresh, "Achieve much more" - it just goes on and on!

Is there any purpose, when you're feeling insecure,
To push yourself, or lie awake, when you can't do any more?
To have that constant, gnawing doubt "How long will I survive?
There's just no way to do it all, no matter how I strive."

It's like a hamster's treadmill, except with me inside.
Straining to meet my targets, but, no matter how I've tried
They're out of reach, beyond my scope, impossible to meet.
I feel like throwing in the towel: to just admit defeat.

The thought of simply walking out, and not returning there
Has great appeal. The way I feel, I really would not care
If I never came back where I've been for half my working life.
I'd do it now, if single, but God has blessed me with a wife.

And we are facing this together, as we have been all along;
We've faced our problems hand in hand; together we are strong.
There's a special bond between us - more than a child has with his mother -
With our marriage built on faith, and trust, in God and in each other.

*

POTENTIAL REDUNDANCY

Many of us face, or will face, the threat of redundancy in today's fast evolving world, where what worked yesterday is no longer adequate for today. Following a buy-out of where I worked, I felt I was facing this and was angry that over 20 years of my life, with accumulated experiences and knowledge, could potentially be thrown away.

There is no room for bitterness, there is no room for hate
Just because my role is deemed "Past its sell by date"
This does not mean I'm worthless now, nor that somehow I have failed,
But businesses have to evolve, with some activities curtailed.

Decisions taken from afar will affect our daily lives;
And not just us but families too - our husbands and our wives.
Our homes include our children, in whose lives we're called to share,
And often aged parents, for whom we're called to care.

If I become resentful, bitterness will build within.
Bitterness will lead to hate, and the Bible calls that "Sin."
Forgiveness is an attitude that we are called to show;
Forget past hurts, and present ones, and simply "Let them go."

Move on from feeling angry, advance to the next stage
God has a better plan for you, no matter what your age.
Take stock of what you're good at, and review what you can do:
Not just the things you've always done, but think what makes you "You".

*

WHAT THEN, O LORD?

All Christians agree that Jesus is coming back; one of the issues about which we do not have a common position is what reaction He will have concerning His Church. I offer this, written in March 2001, to stir us up.

When Christian people walk away, and do not fight for God;
When the Church is full of apathetic men.
When those professing Jesus Christ refuse to speak for Him,
What then, O Lord, what then?

When Christians opt to turn their heads, and decide to walk away,
When believers choose to close their eyes to sin.
When Christian leaders tell the world that judgment is not real,
What then, O Lord, what then?

When we ignore the hurting world, so we can focus on ourselves,
When we forget about the widowed and the poor.
When we forget about the starving, and we fill our plates instead,
What then, O Lord, what then?

When the lonely are forgotten, and the prisoners without hope,
When we pious spend our days self-righteously.
When we preserve our buildings but neglect the Father's heart,
What then, O Lord, what then?

When the Saviour says "Enough of this" and comes back to claim His world,
When Jesus Christ returns in holy wrath.
When those who have neglected all the warnings they've been given . . .
What then, O Lord, what then?

Will we all face the judgment Jesus promised will arrive?
Will we all face the judgment seat of Christ?
Will He tell us then He never even knew us by our names?
And what then, O Lord, what then?

*

WHEN!!

Sometimes I get things out of perspective, on other occasions I worry for more realistic reasons.

God understands, and in Psalm 46 verse 10 He tells us to "Be still and know that I am God" - a verse that has come to mean so much to me over the years.

When your mind is spinning endlessly, and your brain just cannot rest;
When you lie awake for hours on end, feeling worried and depressed;
Or when you feel the pain of others, which in turn makes you distressed;
Listen: "Peace, be still!"

When the world around seems hostile, and the pressures seem too great;
When your children are demanding, and are not prepared to wait;
Or when some deadlines are approaching, and you've left it far too late;
Listen: "Peace, be still!"

When all around is chaos, and when you feel the same within;
When you feel your world is insecure, and you feel like giving in;
Or when you have a crisis looming, thinking "Where do I begin?"
Listen: "Peace, be still!"

When there seems to be no avenue that as yet you have not tried;
When your problems are not lessened, but instead are multiplied;
Or when your tear ducts become empty due to all the tears you've cried;
Listen: "Peace, be still!"

It is only when we step aside, or we stop our daily grind;
It is only when we cease to strive that our minds slowly unwind;
It is only then, amidst the rush that we can ever find
True peace, and be still.

*

December 2001

COWARDICE (IN THE FACE OF OTHERS)

This had been on my computer for ages, and I thought it needed finishing: I now think it says what God wanted when I wrote it in 2005: at least it challenged me again when I reread it.

Please excuse the strong language in the last verse, but that reflects, I believe, the way many view "ladies of the streets".

I am ducking responsibility, and I am hiding myself from view.

There's simply no way, here on God's earth, that I'll do what I ought to do.

Sure I'll speak out against hate and injustice - each Sunday in Church, without fear

But not "in the world", to those who have power - there's a danger that someone might hear.

I am rightly indignant for those with no home, no hope and no aspiration.

It's a slight on this land, an affront to our Lord, that such things exist in our nation.

If we are offended by things that we see, on our doorsteps, right close at hand;

God's promises are that if we repent, He will hear and restore this land.

But God's calling to us isn't simply to ask "Lord please put things right in our nation"
Repentance means we acknowledge to God, our role in this situation.
We confess before God there are things we've not done to challenge injustice we see,
And say "Lord here I am, please equip me to serve. What are You wanting from me?"

"What particular call have You laid on my life? Lord I ask that this be revealed.
Do you want me to serve the people around, or are You sending me further afield?
Is Your call on my life to comfort the old, or befriend the "downs and the outs"
To show to the world, and also the Church, that You care for the "withs" and "withouts"?

To swallow my pride and seek out the drunks, the addicts, the homeless, the whores -
Who most middle-class, if given a choice, would reject as "An affront to our shores"
To get down in the gutter with those without hope, to share in their joys and their sorrow
And help them to know, whatever their past, that You have a plan for tomorrow?"

*

ONE DAY

The first verse of this sat on my computer for well over a year, and then on June 22, 2003 it just seemed to fall into place.

One day I'll meet my Jesus and I'll fall down at His feet.
One day I'll meet my Jesus, when my life on earth's complete.
One day I'll meet my Jesus and I hope to hear Him say
"Welcome, good and faithful one, I've been waiting for this day!

Your place is booked in heaven, with all your closest friends.
You can recollect old memories, for time here never ends.
You can sit around the Father's throne, forgiven and restored
And celebrate eternal life, forever with the Lord"

One day I'll meet my Jesus, and I'll know as I am known.
One day I'll meet my Jesus, and I'll stand before the throne,
Where Father God will look at me, and I trust I'll hear Him say
"Through the blood of Jesus Christ, your sins are washed away.

Your place is here in heaven now, with all your closest friends.
You can recollect old memories, for time here never ends.
You can sit around My golden throne, forgiven and restored
And celebrate eternal life, forever with your Lord"

One day I'll meet my Jesus, and I'll know His power within,
One day I'll meet my Jesus, and be no longer slave to sin.
For my home will always be with Him, as I dwell in heaven above -
Surrounded by His angels and surrounded by His love.

"Your place is here, in heaven, with all your closest friends.
We can recollect old memories, for time here never ends.
We can all sit round the golden throne, forgiven and restored
And celebrate eternal life, for now you've met your Lord"

*

ANSWER WHEN HE CALLS

I have often said that all I write is somehow autobiographical, having its roots in my experience or my feelings. That applies to this poem written in July 2001: I sometimes get embarrassed by my own apathy.

The King of Kings is calling me. the Lord of Lords is waiting.
So why do I keep holding back? Why am I hesitating?
Am I afraid of what He'll ask, afraid of His direction?
But where Christ sends He promises He will give me His protection.

He wants to do far more with me than I could dream or ask.
He will give me all the gifts I need for each allotted task.
Are my horizons too restricted? Do I only have man's vision?
Or will I see God's greater plan? And trust for His provision?

If I keep holding back through fear, just what am I neglecting?
God's greater plans and His designs are what I am rejecting.
If I do, and then stagnate, as God's chances pass me by
I have no right to turn to Him, or to ask the question "Why"?

*

THERE'S A BATTLE OUTSIDE RAGING

This sat on my computer for several years until, on the day of the wedding of Prince William and Catherine Middleton, I had ideas how to close it off (not that the wedding had anything to do with the poem)

There's a battle outside raging, and a world that doesn't care
That shows no urge to get involved, to remedy despair.
That couldn't really give a toss when folk are tossed aside
And stripped of all their dignity, humanity and pride.

There's a battle outside raging, and a church that's slow to act
On a call from Christ to `get involved`, and that just ignores the fact:
This world is full of broken lives which <u>we</u> are called to mend;
<u>We</u> are the ones that Jesus chose, the ones He chose to send.

There's a battle outside raging, and a Christ who knows us all
He calls us to be like watchmen, posted upon the wall:
His world's in need of healing, of forgiveness and of love
And the power to act is given us - Christ sends it from above.

The Holy Spirit guides us, if we will let Him have His way:
He will show us each our calling, He will tell us what to say.
He will lead us into conflict with the spirits of this age
But we will emerge victorious, for the world is God's own stage.

There's a battle outside raging, it's to win the souls of men:
To change their lives forever, so they need never sin again.
So men can face their maker with love, not fear, inside
Because they have met their Saviour, for they are why He died.

*

Then sings my soul, my Saviour God to Thee
"How great Thou art, how great Thou art."
Then sings my soul, my Saviour God to Thee
"How great Thou art, how great Thou art."

Words by Stuart K Hine

IF MARY HAD SAID "NO"

Most Christian traditions honour Mary, the mother of our Lord, some more than others. All respect her for her obedience. In the build up to Christmas 2002 I wondered what would have happened if she had said "No"?

"Mary" came the angel's voice, "Mary you've been chosen
To bear the Saviour of the world" - but Mary's heart was frozen,
Locked in ice, as cold as night, God's call to her ignored:
So God's plan to save mankind could never be secured.

The Devil now possessed the earth, for sin had no redemption:
Hell was each man's destiny; there could be no exemption.
Man was helpless in the face of Hell's lying and deceit
For in Mary's frozen heart, God had met His first defeat.

From the foundation of the earth God had sought a willing heart
To be the mother of His Son: someone special, set apart.
And Mary was that chosen one: a pure and honest child
Who trusted God and worshipped Him, and on whom the Father smiled.

So when the Virgin turned her back, and refused to bear God's Son
All Hell broke loose upon the earth, for the Devil knew he'd won.
All mankind was his to rule, now God had been defied
Then God the Father turned away, and hung His head -
and cried.

*

A CHRISTMAS REFLECTION

On Christmas Day 2010 the Church where Gwen and I worship shared the service with friends from the 7ᵗʰ Day Adventists. Although they celebrate the fact of Christ's birth, the 7ᵗʰ day Adventists do not celebrate December 25ᵗʰ in the same way as we do, as Biblically this cannot be proven to be the day of His birth.
I wanted something slightly different, which brought the Christian cycle together, to open the service, and came up with this.

Hush, can you hear how He does, it? How God breaks into His world?
Not with a blast on the trumpet, or with heavenly banner unfurled.
But in the squalor and chaos, an innocent virgin gives birth
And God, reaching down from His Heaven, dwells with His people on earth.

And we, looking back through the ages, worship the babe she adored
For that child lying there in the manger, is Jesus our heavenly Lord.
Whose hands, and whose feet, bore the nail prints as He hung on the cross and He died.
When He rose from the grave - undefeated - the whole host of Hell was denied.

But just Christmas and Easter together are not the whole of God's plan
For God has a bigger agenda - the total redemption of man
From the sin that began in the Garden, where Satan caused Adam to fall:
And our Saviour, our Lord, our Redeemer, is the babe lying there in the stall.

So come and gaze on your Saviour, draw near and worship Him there
In that stable with donkeys and cattle, and with Mary that virgin so fair:
That baby conceived by God's Spirit, a manger His first earthly bed.
So come, and follow the Magi, to the place where that bright star has led.

*

THE JUDGEMENT SEAT

When you stand before the Judgment seat, what excuses
will you bring?
"Our Church went through division?
And we never had a mission,
For our Elders had no vision?"
When you stand before the Judgment seat, what excuses
will you bring?

When you stand before the Judgment seat, what baggage
will you bring?
The sins still not surmounted?
The hurts to you - all counted?
God's love for you - discounted?
When you stand before the Judgment seat, what baggage
will you bring?

When you stand before the Judgment seat, what friends
will greet you there?
The friends who prayed for you for years?
The friends who prayed for you with tears?
The friends who helped you face your fears?
When you stand before the Judgment seat, what friends
will greet you there?

When you stand before the Judgment seat, what trophies
will you bring?
The lives that you've affected?
The people redirected?
From God's purpose not deflected?
When you stand before the Judgment seat, what trophies
will you bring?

When you stand before the Judgment seat, what will the Father see?
A soul who knew why Jesus came?
A soul released from sin and shame?
A soul set free in Jesus name?
When you stand before the Judgment seat, what will the Father see?

*

PETER'S MAUNDY THURSDAY

*One night in the week before Easter 2001 I could not sleep,
as there was a massive audit looming at work. At around
2.00 in the morning I gave up, went downstairs and read
the Maundy Thursday/Good Friday narrative. At that
time, I could empathise with Peter as never before . . .*

The crowing cock cut through his heart, his world
collapsing fast:
He had betrayed the Son of God: was "the future" now
"the past"?
Had all his dreams gone up in smoke as they took his
Lord away
To face a judge and jury on that dread Passover Day?
What could he do, what could he say? He had betrayed
Him thrice:
Like Christ had said "Peter, you will, before the cock
crows twice."
And at that very moment when those fateful words were
said
Jesus did not say a word - He simply turned His head.

No way could he hold back the tears once he'd looked in
Jesu's eyes:
Three times around the courtyard they had seen through
his disguise.
Three times he had been challenged and said he'd never
known "that man"
So what was left, now that He'd gone? What was left of
His great plan?

He'd had a mission, that's for sure: success seemed very near:
He'd dealt with sin a different way - with forgiveness, not with fear;
He'd shown that God could deal with men by changing what's inside,
If only they had listened . . . ., if only they had tried
To follow in the way He'd led, or to give His way a chance.
But now? Without a future, and without a backward glance
Peter crept into the shadows, and cried until his ducts were dry,
And called out, between his heaving sobs "Why, my Jesus? Why?"

"Why did I fail the final test, as You were led away?
Why did I ever come here, and what prompted me to stay?
I wish that I could take Your place, I no longer want to live.
And all I want, before I die, is to know that You forgive."

*

THE CRUCIFIXION

The Crucifixion is the pivotal point of history: and was the only time that our Lord was separated from His Father, and from the Holy Spirit.

Thank God for Calvary.

As is often the case, this sat on my computer, half finished, for many months until one night in May 2004 I suddenly knew how to close it.

The sun beat down from a cloudless sky;
The birds, their singing stilled.
The ground stained red from holy blood
As the Son of God was killed.

The cross was rough, the nails were coarse
The soldiers coarser still,
When the Lamb of God came forth to die
Upon that bloodstained hill.

The sounds of whipping now were past,
Those weals were fresh, and sore.
His skin was flayed from back and legs
God's Son could take no more.

They nailed Him to that awful cross,
Impaled through hands and feet.
Then hung Him 'neath that cloudless sky
Humiliation now complete.

The Son of God still prayed for those
Who'd plotted for His death.
He asked the Father to forgive
With pain-filled, gasping breath.

And as He hung upon that cross
His Father, on His throne,
Turned away from Jesus Christ:-
And Jesus was alone.

*

THE COVENANT 2003

Once again in December 2002, I could not sleep, so I sat down to write: originally this was to be about the real meaning of Christmas, but it seemed to take its own course as I wrote.

Could you feel it, could you touch it, could you hold it in your hand?
Could you sense the joy of Christmas all around?
Was there a real, deeper, meaning to all the tinsel and the lights?
And has the Jesus, once forgotten, now been found?

Do the values of the world now seem so abstract and remote?
Does the way you used to live now bring you pain?
For you crossed the bridge from sin into a life of joy and peace
The moment you allowed your Lord to reign.

Your life's no longer yours to own, it belongs now to the King
Who laid down His life two thousand years ago.
And your response to what He did? Is it obedience to His voice?
And where He leads are you prepared to go?

For this Christian life we share means we have freedom
under Christ:
This freedom bought at such tremendous cost.
But there are many hurting people who do not acknowledge
Jesus Christ -
Though Jesus came to seek and save the lost.

As you rededicate yourself to the service of your Lord
Do you recognise His place upon the throne?
Can you say, and really mean it, "Jesus put me where You
will"?
For you belong, my precious friend, to Him alone.

*

WHY DO WE NOT GET EXCITED??

During one of the times of quiet in the Covenant Service in January 2005 I started to think about Calvary: with all that Jesus suffered for us so we could have our sins forgiven, why do we so often fail to be excited?

As He spread His hands to take the nails so cruelly driven in
The blood that flowed from hands and feet brought cleansing from our sin.
With open wounds that scarred His back, and the vicious crown of thorn
Jesus Christ gave up His life, midst ridicule and scorn.

That free forgiveness that He bought: do we <u>really</u> understand
What Jesus suffered with the nails that shattered feet and hand?
Do we <u>really</u> understand the cost to have our sins forgiven?
Have we any concept of His pain - cut off from God in heaven?

Can we feel his deep rejection when the Father turned away
And left Him, naked, on the cross, that dread - but glorious - day?
When the hosts of heaven abandoned Him, they could not bear to see
Jesus, filthy with our sin, as He bled for you and me.

Can we imagine what the Saviour felt? Can we conceive His loss?
As eternal battles raged around that awful blood stained Cross?
Abandoned by His Father, and by the angel hosts as well
Which left the way wide open then, for all the hosts of Hell?

Jesus spoke but seven times when hanging on that cross,
And each of us is Jesu's gain, and each the devil's loss.
"Into Your hands" our Saviour cried, then died there, - broken-hearted;
But not before His triumph shout *"It is over, what I started!"*

*

MAKE TIME

In our lives many of us are constantly on the go - and suffer from a misplaced feeling of guilt if we sit down and relax, or indulge in our hobbies. It is important that we make time for ourselves, to recharge our batteries, in order to be ready for whatever life may throw at us. In doing so, however, we must not forget others both inside, and outside, our families.

The `core` of this had sat on my computer for five years, until I had some inspiration on how to complete it on 28th December 2010, the day my Mother died.

Make time to smell the roses as you pass along life's way;
Make certain you make time for rest, and that you make the time for play.
Enjoy the world that God has given, and enjoy His people too
We were created for His pleasure, and that means me and you.

Make time for acts of kindness, helping others in their need,
Touch them where they're hurting, and bandage where they bleed.
Let your hands be hands of healing as you go the extra mile
And where people are in conflict, go and help them reconcile.

Make time to listen carefully when others need to speak:
True strength is shown in listening to the people who feel weak.
Where life has dealt an unfair hand, where pain and hurt abound,
Is where our Lord commanded that His people should be found.

Make time to see your children as they develop and they grow:
If you miss out on their childhood, then it won't be you they know.
It will be `another mother` in whose care and charge they grew
And when they call for `Mummy` - will it be her, instead of you?

Make time for all your loved ones. Tell your parents that you care:
For in our lives there comes a time when our parents won't be there.
The ones who watched and helped us as we'd stumble and we'd fall:
It will be too late to tell them that we loved them after all.

Make time to hear the Father when you come to Him in prayer:
And come to Him with boldness, for the Father's always there.
He will make the time to listen then He'll spend a while with you
So you're equipped to go and do what God would have you do.

*

THE BLOOD THAT JESUS SHED

*Why are we so reticent these days to talk about the Blood
of Jesus? Our spiritual forebears were not afraid of this
subject, and those of us who have seen, or experienced,
spiritual deliverance, will appreciate the power that
Jesus' blood still has today.*

Has the blood that Jesus shed for you fully cleansed your
mortal soul?
Has the fact that Jesus bled for you really made you whole?
Has the fact He chose to lay aside all the joys that Heaven
could give
And chose to come and die for you, really changed the
way you live?

Do you know the power of Jesu's blood, which cleanses
man from sin?
Have you stepped into the crimson flood - or are you
frightened to get in?
Have you felt the flush of purity as your sins are swept aside
By the awesome power of Jesu's blood, by that surging
crimson tide?

Why does the blood of Jesus have this power beyond
compare?
What was it in the Son of God, in whose life we're called
to share?
It's not that Jesus loved us all before the world begun
But it's simply that He chose to die - as the only sinless
one.

The blood that Jesus chose to shed, two thousand years ago
Still has the power to change our lives, as we step into the flow.
As we take our place with Mary, and gaze on His broken form
And feel those drops of holy blood; holy blood still wet and warm.

Pure blood from a pure sacrifice, pure blood not stained by sin.
Pure blood poured out upon that cross, which will let those sinners in
To share with Christ the joys of Heaven, who have known the second birth:-
To prepare us to return with Him - to reclaim and cleanse this earth.

*

September 2001

AN EMPTY CROSS

Many Catholic churches have a cross with an image of Christ on it at the front. Where Gwen and I worship there is an empty cross on the front wall: In January 2002 I wondered why . . .

There's an empty cross upon the wall that talks of Jesu's death:-
Of how He died, and where He cried - as He drew His dying breath
"It is over, it is done, the work for which I came:-
Satan crushed, his power destroyed, through the power of My name."

There's an empty cross upon the wall that confirms the empty tomb:-
An empty cross that spreads the light that pierces through the gloom.
That gives the power to change men's lives, to bring man close to God:-
Satan crushed, his power destroyed by the path that Jesus trod.

There's an empty cross upon the wall that promises new life:-
It's an empty cross that spells the end for hate, and war, and strife.
"I have triumphed" Jesus said, "My work has been achieved:-
Satan crushed, his power destroyed for all who will believe."

There's an empty cross upon the wall, where redemption can be found:-
The blood of Christ, still wet, still warm, still saturates the ground
On which we walk when we approach the cross on which He died:-
Satan crushed, his power destroyed, when we are purified.

*

CRUCIFIED - BY ME?

Can you see Him hanging on the cross? My sin helped
put Him there.
My anger and my bitterness,
Complacent where I saw distress,
Seeking only my own success.
What's more I didn't care.

Can you see His naked body now? My sin helped put it
there.
The times I stole, the times I lied.
My selfishness, my foolish pride
I didn't even try to hide.
What's more I didn't care.

Can you see the nails with blood stains now? I helped to
bang them in.
My evil thoughts, my wicked mind.
My actions, often so unkind
Ignoring deaf, and lame, and blind
What's more, I didn't care.

Can you see the tomb is empty now? My Father raised
His Son.
No crown of thorns upon His brow,
The power of sin is broken now:
The future seems so bright, somehow,
What's more, I really care.

*

January 2002

PENTECOST: WHAT WILL IT BRING?

When I read the Bible I have the advantage of knowing the outcome of the events, but at the time there must have been uncertainty for those involved. How did the disciples feel as they waited, after the Ascension??

"Why did You have to do it, Jesus, why did You have to go
Back into the heavens, Jesus, and leave us here below
To face an angry crowd, Jesus, who scourged and murdered You?
Why did You have to leave, Jesus, what are we going to do?"

"You will be My witnesses, and spread God's word abroad"
But we are simple, unschooled men; how can we do this, Lord?
How can we take the truth of God to those who won't believe?
We need You here beside us, Jesus, why did You have to leave?

"Stay in the city", we were told, "Till the appointed hour
When the Promise of the Father comes to clothe you all with power".
What is this Promise, Jesus, that will help us reach the lost?
Why won't You answer, Jesus, on this feast of Pentecost?

*

WHAT KIND OF JESUS?

*I was leading worship one day at Kennington URC/
Methodist Church in March 2011, when we used the song
"Open our eyes, Lord, we want to see Jesus": I asked the
congregation what kind of Jesus did they want to see, and
it struck me that I had never answered that question for
myself. I wrote this potentially to answer the question in
my own mind.*

What kind of Jesus do you see as you come to Him in
prayer?
The Jesus of compassion, who always seems to care?
Or the Jesus who assures us that "I am always there"?
How do you see Jesus?

What kind of Jesus do you see, as you sit there in your
room?
The baby Jesus, newly born, fresh from Mary's womb?
Or the triumphant risen Saviour, bursting from the
tomb?
How do you see Jesus?

What kind of Jesus do you see, when you see Him
crucified?
The broken Jesus, whipped and scarred, who hung His
head and died?
Or the Jesus now with royal crown, sat at His Father's
side?
How do you see Jesus?

What kind of Jesus do you see when you start to look within?
The Jesus who, with piercing eyes, exposes all your sin?
Or the Jesus who, at Heaven's doors, welcomes sinners in?
How do you see Jesus?

What kind of Jesus do you see when you look into His eyes?
The man who cleansed the Temple? The child who spoke there with the wise?
Or the Christ who faced the devil, and who saw through his disguise?
How do you see Jesus?

However you see Jesus there is always more to know,
For Jesus comes in many ways to sinners here below.
And when you join the hosts in Heaven then you will truly know
The glory that is Jesus.

*

THE CALL

On July 13th 2002 in Reading there was a gathering of mainly young Christians for a day of prayer and fasting for the country. Gwen and I went to Hythe Road Baptist Church, Ashford, that day to join with others who had not been able to make the trip. During a time of worship, when we could hear police sirens and fire engine bells going along the road, the following came to me:-

We could hear the sirens wailing as we stood before the throne
And the Father revelled in the worship of the gathered ones: His own.
As we gazed upon Christ's wounded feet, and we held His nail pierced hand
We could hear the Father as He spoke, and He said "I understand."
"I understand the cry you make, for the youth and for this land;
But I call you first not to advance, but I call you first to stand.
To stand against oppression, and to stand against the flow
Which is sweeping all before it, who have nowhere else to go.
To stand against the spirit which corrupts your nation's youth:
To stand upon the solid rock: proclaiming "Jesus is the truth".

*

It is easy to write: but not so easy to do!

"Come, now is the time to worship.
Come, now is the time to give your heart.
Come, just as you are to worship.
Come just as you are before your God.
Come!"

Words by Brian Doersken

MARY'S CHILD, SON OF GOD

A few years ago I wrote some songs for our Departmental Christmas party at work that were based around well known Christmas songs. They seemed to go down very well, so I wondered if I could write anything appropriate for worship.
This is to the tune "Jingle bells", and (for those trying to sing it) has verse, chorus, verse, chorus, verse, chorus, chorus.

Songs of praise were heard, arcing right across the skies:
"Jesus has been born and in a manger lies".
Shepherds left their flocks and to the stable ran
The first to see the Son of God now become a man.

> *Mary's child, Son of God, in the manger lay,*
> *Is the one we worship now, on this Christmas Day.*
> *Angels sang, shepherds ran to the manger bare:-*
> *Gazing at the infant child, they knelt and worshipped there.*

None has ever seen a child so full of grace,
When we look at You, we see the Father's face.
Lord we come to see, not just the new born child
But the man the Father loved - pure and undefiled.

> *Mary's child, Son of God, make us more like You,*
> *Let us show the Saviour now in all we say or do.*
> *Mary's child, Son of God, we kneel at Your feet:*
> *Jesus at the centre, can make our lives complete.*

Angels sang their songs, bringing worship to the King.
Wise men travelled far, all their gifts to bring.
We would offer too, all we have to give
To the One who came to die, so that we might live.

Mary's child, Son of God, came to earth for me
Born that day in Bethlehem, died at Calvary.
Paid the price, by Your death I have been set free,
All my sins forgiven now, thanks to Calvary.

Mary's child, Son of God, risen now to reign,
Born a babe in Bethlehem, You will come again.
Mary's child, Living Lord, live in us, we pray
For our lives have purpose now, thanks to Christmas
Day.

*

To the tune "Jingle Bells"

WORSHIP JESUS

Sometimes I just get carried away with ideas: I wanted to play "Love me Tender" on the saxophone, but found I could not (that is not unusual, I generally find I can't play anything but hymns and choruses), so I put some Christian words to what is a very lovely melody

Worship Jesus, only Him, take Him as your King
When you see His nail scarred hands, give Him everything
Worship Jesus, Him alone, nothing else will do,
For you know at Calvary, Jesus died for you.

Worship Jesus, day by day, from your past set free.
All your sins and guilt are gone, cleansed at Calvary.
Worship Jesus, praise His name, lift His name on high
He is risen from the grave, never more to die.

Worship Jesus, see His hands, see His feet as well
Nail scarred hands and nail scarred feet, broke the pow'r of Hell.
Worship Jesus, see His head, once with crown of thorn -
He burst forth from death's domain, that first Easter morn.

Worship Jesus, think on Him, worship and adore
House and home and family, should not come before.
Worship Jesus, worship Him, God come down as man;
Opening your path to God: God's eternal plan.

*

COME AND DRINK

I was thinking about the "I Am" sayings of Jesus, and their meaning to us,and these first two verses flowed immediately. I had envisaged it being sung to a simple "lilting air", such as below, to which I created the very simple melody line and Hugh Burnham added the chords for me. Please feel free to make up a tune that fits your worship pattern: we know of a large Baptist Church in the South East of England who use this during communion, sung to a tune composed by a gifted friend of ours.

Come and drink from the living fountain,
Come and drink for this water's free.
Come and drink from the living fountain,
Come and drink of Me.

Come and eat of the bread eternal,
Come and take of the life I give.
Come and eat at the Master's table,
Come and eat - and live.

Come and have all your sins forgiven,
Come, you can have your life restored.
Come and sit at the feet of Jesus,
Listen to your Lord.

Come be filled with the Holy Spirit,
Come be touched by the living flame.
Come and receive the Father's Promise,
Come - He calls your name.

COME AND DRINK

A LILTING AIR

WELL DONE, THOU GOOD AND FAITHFUL SERVANT

The school I attended, the Duke Of York's Royal Military School, has proud traditions, and is one of the few schools to have as its School Hymn one especially written for it. The words, and the tune, "Sons of the Brave" epitomise the ethos of the school, and I have used the tune in this hymn, written in 1985 shortly after attending Spring Harvest when the classic "The Servant King" was first sung.

"Well done, thou good and faithful Servant."
Was said of You, Lord Jesus Christ,
When You gave all You had for others,
And all ambitions sacrificed.
Servant of all, You're our example.
Servant of all, we know You would
Have us approach Your throne, each asking
"Give us the gift of servanthood".

"Well done, thou good and faithful servant."
I beg You, say that Lord of me.
My pride, my status and desires
Laid on the Cross of Calvary.
Servant of all, You have permission
Servant of all, to convince me
Along with all Your other servants
In servanthood we can be free.

"Well done, thou good and faithful servant."
I pray I hear that Lord, from You.
When I stand at the gates of heaven
And hear You say "Come: enter through".
Servant of all, I beg You take me
Servant of all, my whole life through;
And let me show by serving others -
My object is to follow You.

"Well done, thou good and faithful Servant."
Jesus, You showed us how to serve.
We cannot fail to heed Your message
If we, Your life closely observe.
Servant of all, was Your life's purpose,
Servant of all, from start to end.
You came, to humble, poor beginnings
And died our Servant, Saviour, Friend.

To the tune:- "Sons of the Brave".

*

SONS OF THE BRAVE

School Hymn of the Duke of York's Royal Military School, Dover

Reproduced with permission

JESUS CHRIST NOW REIGNS IN GLORY

I have been learning the saxophone for a few years now: from my schooldays I can still hear the band playing "Men of Harlech" as we marched around the parade square, so that was a tune I wanted to learn: I was soon tempted to put words to it.

Jesus Christ now reigns in glory. History was all His story.
He will reign forever more, He sits at God's right hand.
From our hearts our praise ascending, with the angel voices blending,
Bringing worship never ending to our heav'nly King!

From heaven He descended!
To heaven He ascended!
There to reign eternally,
For Satan's power here on earth is ended.

Chorus:-
Jesus Christ now reign in glory,
History was all Your story.
Countless numbers bow before Thee
Jesus Christ, our King!

Angels join in celebration, men from ev'ry age and nation.
Voices raised in adoration of our heav'nly King.
Christ, Your mercy ever showing; wonder in our hearts is growing,
Adoration over-flowing to our heav'nly King!

Hymns of praise ascending.
Spirit's power descending
On you and me so we can be
Part of the army Jesus Christ is sending.

Chorus:-
Jesus Christ now reign in glory,
History was all Your story.
Countless numbers bow before Thee
Jesus Christ, our King!

*

2005

TO YOUR CROSS

In November 2001 I was thinking about the Annual Covenant Service, and the depth of the Methodist Covenant Prayer seemed to resound in my mind at the same time as the hymn "The Old Rugged Cross" - so I have tried to join them together. Whilst it was first being sung at the Covenant Service at the Centrepiece Church, Ashford, in January 2002 I wanted to make changes, but I have been persuaded to leave it as it is.

Lord I come to Your cross, bring myself once again
And I give You the whole of my heart.
For I ask You, dear Lord, to accept me once more
And help me to make a new start.

Jesus take me and make me anew
Fill me up with Your Spirit again.
You've been with me in all I've gone through,
And just praying I'd give You my pain.

I have failed You, dear Lord, I have been insincere.
I have slipped, I have fallen away.
I have doubted Your word, I have criticised those
Who have met You a different way.

Jesus take me and make me anew
Fill me up with Your Spirit again.
You've been with me in all I've gone through,
And just praying I'd give You my pain.

With my past in Your hands, all my hurts and my fears,
I know, Lord, I can be complete.
All I was, all I am, and Lord all I will be
I bring and I place at Your feet.

Jesus take me and make me anew,
Fill me up with Your Spirit again.
You've been with me in all I've gone through,
And just praying I'd give You my pain.

Where You want I will move, what You send I will do,
My future I bring to Your throne:
All my dreams, my desires, all the plans I have made,
For I can be no longer my own.

Jesus take me and make me anew,
Fill me up with Your Spirit again.
Give me Your pow'r and give me Your love,
To share Jesus, the Saviour, with men.

To the tune ` The old rugged cross`

*

THEY PUT NAILS

In 2005 I wanted something to describe the scene when the Disciples saw the risen Lord for the first time, but could not find anything suitable, so I wrote this to the tune: "Give me oil in my lamp"

"They put nails in My hands when they killed Me,
And a nail through My feet as well.
With a spear in My side to confirm it:-
I was dead as anyone could tell."

Chorus
"I have risen, I have risen
I have risen from the stone-cold tomb.
I have risen, I have risen
I have risen from the tomb."

"Put your finger in these holes where the nails went;
In these holes that they made in Me:
Put your hand in My side, and believe it
I'm alive again as you can see."

Chorus

"Now you see, you believe: doubt has vanished
For "My Lord and my God", you said.
But more blessed those who say without seeing:-
"Christ my Lord is risen from the dead""

Chorus

*

HONESTY AND INTEGRITY

In September 2006 Hugh Burnham, our guitarist and worship leader at Kennington URC/Methodist Church bemoaned the lack of hymns concerning honesty in daily living. This is set to the tune "Aurelia", usually associated with "The Church's One Foundation".

A world full of confusion, a world full of deceit,
Where promises are broken, and people lie and cheat.
But truth is still among us, God's truth resides within
To keep us straight and honest, to keep His flock from sin.

God's church should be a beacon, a pure and holy light
With ears attuned to heaven, and doing what is right.
Not compromising truth nor allowing shades of grey
But acting like the Saviour in all we do or say.

God's word still stands unchallenged: "Be true in all you are":-
Our words, our thoughts, our actions are seen both near and far.
We must display, unsullied, the Lord we represent
And, as His sons remember, it is by Him we're sent.

Our God expects high standards, no lying or deceit;
Our word must be our bond to the people that we meet.
Our actions, those of Jesus, who was the perfect man -
The total, full completion of heaven's eternal plan.

*

WE GATHER HERE TO PRAISE AND WORSHIP

Hugh Burnham has a lot to answer for! One Sunday in 2006 he wanted to use the hymn "The day Thou gavest, Lord, is ended" but felt the opening verse was not appropriate for a morning service. I originally rewrote the first verse as below, but then I decided I would finish the whole hymn.

We gather here to praise and worship
The Father, Son and Holy Ghost.
Our praise, ascending to the heavens
Blends with that from the angel host.

We praise our Father, the creator
Whose voice the earth both formed, and forms.
And in whose tender arms we shelter
Secure - in Him - from all life's storms.

We praise our Saviour, Lord and Master
Who died for us on Calvary
And rose again, the tomb is empty
Now "Death, where is thy victory"?

We praise the Sprit; God indwelling
His people to bring inner power
To live our lives as God intended
And let God's gifts burst into flower.

We praise the Godhead, God eternal
From before time till time shall cease;
Because we know that in God's heaven
We all shall dwell in perfect peace.

*

FATHER SPEAK FOR WE ARE LISTENING

*I remember Tony Campolo saying one day that when he
prays he often says nothing, he just listens to God. I love
putting words to well known tunes, so one day in 2005
when we were singing "Father hear the prayer we offer",
my mind started to drift to the fact that sometimes prayer
is us speaking, when it should also be God speaking.
I could not, however, come up with a better line to finish
with than is in the original: sheer God-inspired genius.*

Lord, we need to hear You speaking
Spending time just being still:
Let You speak into our hearts, Lord,
And embrace our Father's will.

Father speak for we are listening,
Ears attuned to what You'll say:
And, when we have heard You speaking,
Give us strength, Lord, to obey.

Give us strength to take Your message
To a world ensnared by sin
And, as You embraced us warmly,
Help us bring the seekers in.

Give us, Lord, the eyes of Jesus
So we view Your world with love:
Hating sin but leading sinners
To forgiveness from above.

Give us, too, the ears of Jesus
Listening ears, for others' pain.
Give us, then, the grace of Jesus
Making people whole again.

Lord, we want to be like Jesus;
In our lives be glorified,
And that we may never falter
Father be Thou at our side!

To be sung to the tune "Sussex", usually associated with the hymn "Father hear the prayer we offer".

*

MY JESUS DIED FOR ME

Sometimes I just like playing around with words and/or music. That is how this one, sung to the tune of "God Save the Queen." started in 2006.

My Jesus died for me
That day at Calvary,
King of the Jews.
Nails through His hands and feet,
His sacrifice complete;
I fall now at His feet:
King of the Jews.

His blood was shed for me
That day at Calvary,
Sin to forgive.
I live in certainty
Of Jesu's love for me.
Free for eternity
Now I can live.

His blood that flowed so free
That day at Calvary,
Freedom ensures.
My sin all washed away
On that most glorious day.
Lord Jesus have Your way!
My life is Yours!

*

ABANDONED, FORESAKEN

I had long wanted to write a hymn/song that would come before "Abba, Father" in the books, and in May 2009 I landed on the words "Abandoned, Forsaken", which fitted the opening to the tune St Denio (Joanna) most frequently associated with the old classic hymn "Immortal, Invisible God only Wise". The words just seemed to flow fairly easily after that.

Abandoned, forsaken and whipped till He bled,
Then Jesus, my Saviour, to death He was led.
The death that He suffered at cruel Calvary,
His body was broken for all men to see.

Abandoned, forsaken He hung there and died;
My Jesus, my Saviour, by men crucified.
His hands pierced, His feet pierced, and with crown of thorn
Rejected, subjected to hatred and scorn.

Abandoned, forsaken, but victory won.
For this was the triumph of God's only Son.
Alone, isolated, this disfigured man
Had bought our salvation through God's perfect plan.

Abandoned, forsaken, my Lord chose to die.
He chose that cruel pathway so that you and I
Could know full forgiveness from Heaven above
And live there, forever, in God's perfect love.

*

IT'S A PIECE OF CAKE FOR JESUS

Gwen and I had been listening to some teaching by Andrew Wommack, and one phrase rang out in my ears "It's a piece of cake for Jesus", so I wondered what tune that could be set to, and with the addition of an extra note at the front of each verse it fits very well to "The Battle Hymn of the Republic". Later that week our Minister, Richard Grocott, asked me to lead worship on the theme "Christian Hope", and so the song below was born in a very short time. I apologise for copying the chorus from another hymn, but there is no way I could improve on these words.

It's a piece of cake for Jesus bringing hope to those who mourn;
Whose past was Hell, whose present, grim, whose future looks forlorn.
For with Jesus in the picture there can be a bright new dawn:
With Jesus Christ our King

Praise and glory be to Jesus!
Praise and glory be to Jesus!
Praise and glory be to Jesus!
For Jesus Christ is King.

It's a piece of cake for Jesus bringing hope where there's despair;
The future is a brighter place as long as He is there:
Christ Jesus died to save our souls, and Jesus lives to care:
And Jesus Christ is King

Praise and glory be to Jesus!
Praise and glory be to Jesus!
Praise and glory be to Jesus!
For Jesus Christ is King.

It's a piece of cake for Jesus bringing hope for evermore;
Eternal hope, eternal life upon that Heavenly shore.
For by His death upon the cross He opened heaven's door
Where Jesus Christ is King.

Praise and glory be to Jesus!
Praise and glory be to Jesus!
Praise and glory be to Jesus!
For Jesus Christ is King.

It's a piece of cake for Jesus bringing hope where there is fear;
His name will drive the demons out, and He will linger near.
So sing aloud the glorious words that Satan hates to hear:
That Jesus Christ is King.

Praise and glory be to Jesus!
Praise and glory be to Jesus!
Praise and glory be to Jesus!
For Jesus Christ is King.

*

March 2011

PRAISE YOU JESUS

In July 2003 Gwen and I were talking about nursery rhymes, and I wondered if I could write a praise song for young children to the rhythm of a well known nursery rhyme: it may not be theologically very deep, but it may serve a purpose in a playgroup, reception class or Sunday School.

To the tune of Baa Baa Black Sheep

Praise You, Jesus, we have come to praise.
Praise our Saviour all our days.
Praise for Your goodness, praise for Your love,
Praise You that You came to earth from heav'n above.

Praise You, Jesus, Jesus You're our man!
Lord of water, Lord of land.
Lord of the universe, Lord of the air,
And You're Lord of everything, Lord everywhere.

Love You Jesus, Jesus we love You.
What You ask us, we will do.
Love our neighbour, love our friend,
For the love that Jesus has can never end.

*

"Precious memories, how they linger,
How they ever flood my soul,
In the stillness of the midnight,
Precious, sacred scenes unfold."

The Sullivan Family

CHOIR PRACTICE

This was submitted for the Methodist Church Competition in 2003, and the idea germinated from a distantly remembered piece by Max Boyce where he observed that no Welsh choir ever came last: they may have come ninth out of nine, but never last. This only came second in the Ashford Area, but I like it anyway.

We came far and wide to rehearsals, and everyone always turned up,
Determined to show up the Baptists, and win back the coveted cup.
The cup that was given each Autumn to the church whose choir was best.
No more we'd come second, as this year we reckoned
That we were "simply the best".

We practised like mad through the winter - snow and ice couldn't keep us away.
Though it may sound (to some) we were crazy, we focussed our minds on "that day"
"That day" which was ringed in our diaries, "that day" dominating our lives:
Choir practice, we knew was the thing we could do
To miss watching the soaps with our wives.

Spring brought no respite from our practice, the day drew steadily nigh.

Though maybe our wives felt rejected, they knew better than asking us "Why?"

If they won the Baptists would mock us, we couldn't risk coming in second.

So as day follows night, through darkness and light
Many more practices beckoned.

We'd practise at home in the bathroom, we'd sing it asleep in our bed.

I recall the words of our leader, when after one evening he said:

"Don't be embarrassed, dear colleagues, just sing it wherever you are"

So at West Ham one day, as "Bubbles" floated away
My clear voice rang out "Hallelujah".

At last dawned the day of the contest, our chance to reclaim the prize.

Now, at last, we'd show we were champions:- cut the Baptists right down to size.

We were last to be called to the platform, it seemed like the rest took an age:-

So with throats slaked with honey, and in suits that looked funny
We climbed up onto the stage.

We were ready, and willing, and able. Our chests were
swollen with pride:
We were certain to come out as winners, as "we had God
on our side".
We had practised - it seemed like forever - and knew the
piece inside and out:-
As they drew back the curtain, we all knew for certain
The outcome was never in doubt.

The conductor checked we were ready. He then turned
his face to the band.
The spotlight was trained on his baton, which he held
aloft in one hand.
Then our knees turned to jelly beneath us: our heartbeats
all seeming to cease
As we looked at each other, dismayed to discover
WE HAD PRACTISED THE WRONG BLOOMING
PIECE!

*

HEALTHY EATING

This was the entry for the Methodist Circuit Festival in 2004, written one evening whilst staying in a hotel where the food was anything but `good for the figure`. It won the Ashford and District competition, but I have no idea where it came in the regional finals.

I have a little problem, for I am overweight you see:
Any my wife would like to have a little less of me!
To lose my paunch, my "overhang" is my darling wife's desire:
"In other words, my Husband, get rid of your spare tyre."

"But that's not easy, Dearest, when I spend my days at work
Supervising others, making sure that they don't shirk,
Sitting at my desk all day, working hard as hard can be,
Whilst eating chocolate biscuits and drinking copious cups of tea."

"So put aside those biscuits, and cut down those cups of tea.
You're forty inches round your waist, whilst your hips are thirty three!
Do you want some smart new clothes, cut in the best of taste?
They only look attractive where the hips exceed the waist!

So it's Weetabix for breakfast, (or something of that ilk)
But only single servings, and only ever with skimmed milk.
And there's a lettuce leaf for dinner, with a single Mullerlite,
Carrots will help you lose some weight - and they also aid your sight.

A healthy diet's good for you, to help you shed those pounds;
And despite the mickey taking, the food is nicer than it sounds.
A healthy diet, and exercise, will make you fitter and much stronger
And best of all, (for those you love), it will help you live far longer.

For many years you've gorged yourself on sausage, egg and chips.
While pasta, veg, and wholemeal bread have never passed your lips.
Your favoured diet, you must admit, is truly "sylph" defeating
So put aside your fatty foods, and go in for healthy eating."

"My dear, you've spoken total sense, you've been logical and calm.
A lifestyle change may benefit: at least it can't do any harm.
So for your sake, my Darling, (and also for some peace and quiet),
In just two weeks, I promise you, I'll embrace that healthy diet."

*

AN ODE TO TEETH

Our Dentist in Ashford has had my first book of poems in their waiting room for several years. One day in 2006, when I was waiting for an appointment the receptionist there challenged me to write something new about teeth. Never being one to flinch from a challenge I set to. My wife and I enjoy watching the "Silent Witness" programmes where pathologists identify bodies from dental records, which gave me an idea for the conclusion.

When God made man He took great care
To crown his head with lustrous hair.
Two eyes, two ears, and beneath those
Two nostrils in one - protruding-nose.
Two lips then form a mouth beneath
With God's great gift - two rows of teeth.

The new-born child has none to show
Which, through their childhood slowly grow.
Milk teeth first then - what is scary
Visits next from the Tooth-Fairy
Who, years ago brought a few coppers
When I lost one of my choppers.

Adult teeth then come along
Pearly white - and very strong.
If, with the tooth brush you're not willing
Soon you'll hear the sound of drilling.
So brush them now, without delay
Or God's great gift will soon decay.

Decaying teeth will bring you pain:
The dentist's chair is - once again
Your destiny - so very chilling
Having yet another filling.
Maybe across your mind has flitted
The thought of having false ones fitted.

And, at the end, when life is through
Our teeth will have no more to do:
No veg to chew, no meat to bite,
They can relax now, day and night.
God's gift to man have done their toil
As they rest forever in the soil.

*

CARS

This was written sometime in 1986

I am in the privileged position of having a Company car, and in return the firm insist that I keep it clean - inside and out - on the premise that a clean car is a good advertisement for the firm, and also that a clean car will be cared for more than a dirty one (I won't discuss that idea here).

I can remember when we first had the car - we were out every weekend, assiduously polishing the paintwork and vacuuming inside: that car was a beauty to behold, every mark wiped off immediately, all rubbish cleared out daily - the Transport Director would have been proud of it (and of us)!

Enthusiasm waned as the novelty wore off, however. Honestly, we meant to keep it clean. Other things kept getting in the way, unfortunately. A new baby, increased home, work and church commitments interfered, and imperceptibly but steadily the pristine car became "lived in". It wasn't until I took a close, critical look at it the other day that I realised how far our standards had slipped from where they were when we first had the car.

My reaction was to blitz the outside - the bit that shows, so that anyone looking quickly would think how well kept it was: only the outside was touched, the inside was still a mess, but the car would at least pass a superficial inspection anyway.

How - may I ask you - does your Christian life stand up in comparison to our car cleaning? When you first came to the Lord did you not ensure that both the outside (what the world sees) and the inside (what God sees) were both spotless - any sin, any shortcomings immediately confessed and cleansed away? Was your object not to be spotless, pure and clean at all times?

Has the halo slipped a bit? Do you now concentrate mainly on "the bits that show", on the surface dirt and muck, but the underneath may not be as good as before, and possibly even the surface only gets a "blitz" clean when you take a close look at it.

Try looking inside, at the bits God sees, at your attitudes, at your thoughts, at your relationships, and ask if God is really pleased or not. If He is not, why not try and do something about it?

One reason we have to keep our car clean is that a good, clean car is easier to sell than a neglected one: would anyone buy a second-hand faith from you and make it new for themselves?

*

THE PARABLE OF THE MOWER

This was written in July 1984, and I still like it: what we have seen over the years in the fellowship where Gwen and I worship has borne out the truths in this short passage.

The other week I decided that I should go and mow our lawn, - or rather Gwen decided that I should go and hack my way through our daisies to see if there was any grass hidden there.

Unfortunately the ground was very wet so I had to borrow a friend's hover mower; the sort which skims over the surface of the lawn and cuts the grass sticking up. It was the first time I had ever used one and I was amazed at what happened when I turned it on: it rose up off the lawn and to use it was just like sweeping the grass; it was so quick and easy to use and to stop that it seemed unreal. There are always drawbacks, however, and I noticed that all the clippings were left scattered all over the place, and also that the daisies and dandelions were not cut as close as with our motor mower.

A few days later I went over it again with our motor mower. This seemed like hard work to get it going, to steer it and to stop it when the momentum was under way. The difference in result, however, was dramatic - not a dandelion head or daisy to be seen! Not only that, but all the trimmings and cuttings were neatly gathered in the grass box ready for composting.

I really thought that all the extra effort had been worthwhile until . . . . a few days later the lawn was a mass of bobbing daisy heads again. Where I had just surface trimmed them before they were now sprouting very quickly.

There was nothing for it. Down on hands and knees I went, and I dug out the offending weeds. This was hard work, and it is painful to look at the unsightly, large, brown patches in an otherwise uniform green lawn. The fact that these patches represented places where plants that should not have been present had grown does not make it any easier to look at. If we think, however, we soon realise that where this brown mud is now, there will soon be grass, not weeds, and the whole lawn will benefit from the weeding it was given.

Surely our way of sharing our faith is like grass cutting. There is the quick and easy way which skates way above the surface of the problems, does half a job and leaves debris and broken people all around, just as did the hover mower. It is quick and basically ineffective.

A more thorough approach, as with our motor mower, is harder to do, takes more effort, and is more rewarding. The results are far superior, and we can collect together all those affected, like the cuttings in the grass box. Even this method, however, does not eliminate all problems; some have to be tackled individually, like the weeds.

To tackle problems individually in a fellowship or in any Christian situation, or even in a family, can be very painful. It hurts inwardly to look at our lawn with its bare patches. Similarly it hurts where holes are left where friends fall out, or when people are asked to leave because of their negative influence on the Christian work and witness.

Our lawn will grow again more beautifully than before, and so will the community cleansed in this way - painful though it may be at the time.

Jesus told the Parable of the Sower. I have looked at things from another angle. On reflection I feel that His way is better - but then it usually is.

*

"WERE YOU THERE WHEN THEY CRUCIFIED MY LORD?"

This sketch, first written in 1985, has undergone a couple of rewrites over the years. I am enclosing here the version from 1991.

THE SCENE: An ordinary carpenter's shop, with a workbench and a few tools. A large cross dominates the background:-

Enter Actor **No1** carrying a whip, hammer and nails. He walks past the set, saying (in a nasty voice)
"I can't wait to get on with this one" and goes offstage to where he can be heard but not seen.

Enter Actor **No 2**; walks across set, picks up a hammer:
"Morning Bill"

Enter Actor **No 3**: walks across to join **No 2** at bench
"Morning".

No 2: "What's that going on over there? There's a heck of a din".
No 3 "They're whipping somebody."
No 2: "Anyone we know?"
No 3 "No idea, nothing to do with us. Best to ignore it, I always do."
No 2: "I hear you've got engaged, well done. Nice girl, is she?"
No 3 "Yes, Julie is all I ever wanted: you know the old expression "I worship the ground she walks on"? Well, that is perfectly true in my case."

Enter Actor **No 4**, carrying a set of placards. Goes to the back of the set, to the foot of the cross.

"1 down, 9 to go" hangs up a placard **"No Other Gods"**

Off stage, the sound of whipping.

No 1 (unseen): "Father forgive them, for they know not what they do"

No 2: "What was that he said?"

No 3 "I told you to ignore it, it's the only thing to do."

No 2: "Now what's happening over there?"

No 3 "Looks like they've had their fun with the whip, I think they're going to hang him up now."

No 2: "That's HIS problem. Where are you and Julie going to live after the wedding?"

No 3 "We've got this house, where I'm living now. We're doing it up, and Julie moves in after the big day. Mind you, the place is taking all our time and energy to make it the showpiece it ought to be, and will be - or my name will be mud!"

No 4: "2 down, 8 to go" hangs up a placard **"Make no idols"**

Off stage, the sound of hammering

No 1 (unseen): "Father forgive them, for they know not what they do"

No 2: (startled) "I . . . I heard it again."

No 3 (getting ratty) "Ignore it! Look, can I borrow your hammer?"

Goes to hit the nail, misses and hits his thumb instead, then leaps about in pain.

"GOD! That hurt".

No 4: "3 down, 7 to go":- hangs up a placard **"Do not take my name in vain"**.

Off stage, the sound of hammering

No 1 (unseen): "Father forgive them, for they know not what they do".

No 2: "I . . . no I'll ignore it. Tell me, how are you and Julie passing the time at weekends? Are you seeing a lot of each other?"

No 3 "You must be joking! It's double time working Sunday! How else do you think we're able to pay our mortgage on our dream house?"

No 4: "4 down, 6 to go":- hangs up a placard **"Keep the Sabbath"**

Off stage, the sound of hammering

No 1 (unseen): "Father forgive them, for they know not what they do"

No 2: "Okay, so at the moment you are coping, just, with the extra cash from working Sundays - we all plan our lives around that, don't we? I don't know what Samantha and I would do without it. The trouble is, will that be enough for you, what with the phone bill, council tax, electric etc? Running a house is very pricey, even with overtime."

No 3 "It's okay." My folk are pretty well off, and when they pop off, which shouldn't be long if we're lucky, we'll be really rolling in it. They're not much use to us now, more of a drain on our time and emotions than any use. In fact they'll be more use to us dead than alive"

No 4: "5 down, 5 to go":- hangs up a placard **"Honour thy Parents"**

Off stage, the sound of hammering

No 1 (unseen): "Father forgive them, for they know not what they do"

Enter Actor **No 5**, the Manager's Secretary, looking very depressed:

No 2: "Morning Sandra - and it looks as if you <u>are</u> mourning as well."

No 3 "What's up, love, you don't look your usual self today."

No 4: "I'm pregnant again, and we can't afford it. Even now we can't make ends meet."

No 2: "Does Bill know yet?"

No 4: "No, I haven't dared tell him, he'll be furious when he finds out!"

No 2: "What happened when you went to the Doctors for the result of the test?"

No 4: "They offered me a termination - that's fairly standard for unplanned pregnancies these days, isn't it?"

No 3: "Well, why not go ahead and have one? Who's going to know anyway?"

No 4: "6 down, 4 to go":- hangs up a placard **"Do not kill"**

Off stage, the sound of hammering

No 1 (unseen): "Father forgive them, for they know not what they do"

No 5: "What was that?"

No 3: "Ignore it, you'll soon get used to it:- we both have."

No2: "So Bill doesn't know about your impending problem? Come to think about it, I thought he was dead set against having any more."

No 5: "That's the other problem, it isn't his. Recently he's been a bit distant, a bit morose, and of course he spends a lot of time away on business as well. With all that, we seem to have drifted apart a bit, and one evening this chap started to chat me up - it was all so innocent at first, but one thing led to another - you know how it is these days - and I don't know why but I just didn't want to say "No"."

No 4: "7 down, 3 to go":- hangs up a placard **"Do not commit adultery"**

Off stage, the sound of hammering

No 1 (unseen): "Father forgive them, for they know not what they do"

No 2: "So when will you have it done? You know, the "Op"?

No 5 "I've no idea, I suppose I'll have to make an appointment, but I haven't got the nerve."

No 2: "Well, go on, ring them now, before your nerve finally breaks."

No 5: "I'll have to wait until dinner time, there isn't a phone here."

No 2: "Don't be stupid, the Boss is out for a few hours. You're his Secretary, use your position and his phone. He'll never know."

No 4: "8 down, 2 to go":- hangs up a placard **"Do not steal"**

Off stage, the sound of hammering

No 1 (unseen): "Father forgive them, for they know not what they do"

No 5: "Okay. I'll do it. It seems a good idea, although I'm still not sure. What happens if Bill finds out, he'll kill me."

No2: "That's no problem, leave it to us."

No 5: "What do you mean, "Leave it to us"?"

No 3: "I reckon I know. We'll tell him that this chap told us he got you drunk, totally plastered, by slipping you Mickey Finns all night until you couldn't resist him. You'll be totally in the clear."

No 4: "9 down, 1 to go":- hangs up a placard **"Do not lie"**

Off stage, the sound of hammering

No 1 (unseen): "Father forgive them, for they know not what they do"
No 5 (the Secretary) leaves, looking very downcast and woebegone.

No 2: "I reckon she's a bit of alright. Her husband must be nuts not to look after her properly. In fact with a wife like her, a car like he's got, and that fabulous house in the country - which he's already paid for - he's got it all on a plate. I'd give my right arm for what he's got - all I've got is a council house, a clapped out Skoda and a wife that's only interested in Coronation Street and Neighbours."

No 4: "10 down, none to go":- hangs up a placard **"Do not covet."**

Off stage, the sound of hammering

No 1 (unseen): "Father forgive them, for they know not what they do"

No 3: "Stop dreaming, it's time to knock off. Let's go home and get away from this place for a few hours."
No 2 picks up his tools, both walk slowly to the front of the set.
No 2: "Anyway, who was that chap they kept banging nails into over there?"
No 3: "Forget it. Ignore it. You know it was nothing to do with us."

Both amble slowly off stage, heads down.

*

A MINI SAGA IN 57 WORDS

This was submitted for the Methodist Church Competition in 2003, and was given first place in the whole of the South East of England. The idea was to write a short story in the number of words which represented the number of years the competition had been in existence, so in 2003 the number of words permitted was 57, and in 2004 (on the next page) it was 58 words.

This story does have great sentiment, however, as I well remember our days when we used to watch West Ham in the early years of our marriage. (For our American friends, West Ham play Soccer!)

After the wicked stepsisters departed, Cinderella was all alone, crying over the injustice of it all. Then the Fairy Godmother waved her wand and said "You shall go the ball", at which point Glenn Roeder* came out of the fireplace and said:

"Can the West Ham defence come too? They've not got to the ball all season"

(*At this time, Glen Roeder was the Manager of West Ham United Football Club)

*

A MINI SAGA IN 58 WORDS

In 2004 I entered the "mini saga" competition for the Methodist Circuit Festival: a complete story in 58 words: I decided on a change of style from the humorous entry of the previous year (reproduced on the previous page in this book); this had been rolling around my mind since the last competition in 2003. Much to my surprise this won both the local and the regional competitions.

Friday: She looked; she saw. - The scourged back, the open weals, the mocking crown of thorns.
            She listened; she heard. - The hammered nails, the splintering bones, the insults.
            She wept.

Saturday: She waited. - No more tears left.

Sunday;   She went; she saw. - The open grave, the missing body.
            She wept.
            She listened.
            She heard. - His voice.
            She believed.

*

AND FINALLY: A FEW "ONE-LINERS"

Just occasionally I seem to "invent" a suitable `Bon Mot`, either by inspiration or by a fortunate turn of phrase. No doubt others may have said these before me, and others will do so again, but I include them anyway.

"Do you worship your traditions, or do your traditions help you worship?"

"Do we love the unlovely?"

"Pray **into** the will of God, and then pray **in** the will of God."

"Look back with gratitude, look forward with faith."

My wife often tells me that, because of my expanding waistline, we should use a low fat spread instead of butter. As I tell her, "I don't see why - after all, my waist is now low, it is fat, and it has spread!!"

About my wife, who looks very young for her age, I once remarked that "She is wearing well, whilst I am wearing out".

When asked if we wanted a change of scene, I replied "No thanks, we're fed up, not hard up".

I have often said that "I'm waiting on God" when in reality God is saying "I've been waiting for you."

I once said - not that I believe it - that "Infants have less fun in infancy than adults do in adultery"

Samuel said "Speak, Lord, your servant is listening". How often do we say "Listen, Lord, your servant is speaking"?

I am so jealous of my wife: waking up with me each morning!

Of a lady who was prone to histrionics I once said (and probably shouldn't have done) that "She was highly strung, and should have been."

I was constantly reminded by a friend that I once said, during a sermon, of a particular event that was not well received that it "Went down as well as a pork chop in a synagaogue"

After God healed me from a diagnosis of prostate cancer I said to my wife (paraphrasing Neil Armstrong): "That's a small step for God but a giant step for man".

As Father to the Bride at my eldest daughter's wedding I said in my speech "There are people here who do not believe prayer works. I have news for you - ever since she became a teenager we have been praying she would leave home!".

Finally: It struck me one day that where Gwen and I worship is not strictly Biblical: we have such fun, enjoying worship, and other people's company, each week. This may not seem wrong but didn't Jesus say to Nicodemus "You must be bored again" - or is that just a misunderstanding some churches seem to have taken "on board"(?)

*